W9-CEX-196

Do Mommies Have Mommies?

TIME LIFE for Children ®

ALEXANDRIA, VIRGINIA

Contents

What is a family?

A family can include a father, a mother, sisters, and brothers. Grandparents are part of a family; so are aunts, uncles, and cousins. Every family is different. Some families include people who are not related, but who still care about each other. That's the important thing: Members of a family love each other and want each other to be happy.

Do all children look like their parents?

Some do and some don't. Inside your body are tiny things, called genes, that give your body directions for how you'll look. Genes tell whether your hair will be curly or straight, whether your skin will be dark or light, and whether your eyes will be brown, green, or blue.

Did you know?
A baby's genes come from its mother and father. That's why children often look like their parents. But sometimes genes surprise you. They can make you look like your aunt or uncle—or like no one else in your family at all!

Do mommies have mommies?

Yes, they do! Your mother's mother is called your grandmother; she and your grandfather raised your mother when she was a little girl. Your father's mother and father are your grandparents, too.

Does everyone have a mommy and daddy?

Everyone was once a baby, and every baby was made by a man and a woman together. The baby grew in a special place inside its mother until it was ready to come out. Without a mother and a father, you would not have been born!

Do mommies and daddies always live together?

Not always. Some children live only with their mother or only with their father. Others spend part of the time at their mother's house and part of the time at their father's house. But whether parents live together or apart, they love their children and want them to be happy.

Why don't my grandparents live with me?

When your mother and father were little, they each lived with their own parents. But when your mother and father grew up and got married, they moved into a different home. That's why your grandparents probably live in a different place from you.

Did you know?
In some families, grandparents, aunts, uncles, and cousins all live together. The grownups take turns caring for the children.

Why does Grandpa have gray hair?

As people get older, their bodies change. Their hair turns gray or white; men's hair may even fall out. Also, their skin gets wrinkles and lines. Some older people can't see or hear as well as they used to.

Did you know?
Dogs and cats get gray hair, too!
This usually happens around
their whiskers or nose.

17

What is an aunt?

Your aunt is your mother's sister or your father's sister. Your uncle is your mother's brother or your father's brother. Aunts and uncles can also marry into a family. Ask your parents if you have any aunts or uncles.

Did you know?
The children of your aunt and
uncle are called your cousins.

What happens when a baby is born?

It is a busy time! Just before the baby is born, the mother may go to the hospital so her doctor can take good care of her. Then, after the baby comes home, the parents spend a lot of time taking care of it. A new baby can't talk or walk—it can't even sit up! The baby must be treated very gently.

Did you know?
There's a lot of love in a family.
That's why parents love their
children *and* the new baby.

21

What does "adopted" mean?

One way for a child to come into a family is for the parents to make a baby. Another way is for the child to be adopted. Being adopted means the parents started to take care of the baby after it was born, rather than making a baby themselves. Both ways of joining a family are just as good. They both mean the parents want a child to take care of and love forever.

Why do I have to be nice to my brother?

Because the whole family is happier when the people in it get along. Brothers and sisters love each other, even when they get mad. If you remember that, it will be easier to be nice.

Do bugs have baby brothers?

Many bugs have baby brothers—and sisters—but they've probably never met! That's because most insects don't stay together as a family after the babies are born. And some older bugs look nothing like their baby brothers. When a butterfly hatches from its egg, it looks like a worm. Then it grows a case around itself. When it breaks out of its case, the butterfly looks completely different!

Is my dog in my family?

Your dog is not a person, but in many important ways it is still a member of your family. You love the dog and take care of it, the way people in a family care for each other. You have fun together, the way families do. And your home is the dog's home, too.

Do animals have families?

Most animal parents take care of their babies only until they're strong enough to take care of themselves. But a few wild animals, such as geese, dolphins, wolves, and beavers, do stay together. A beaver family has a mother, a father, youngsters about one year old, and new babies. The family lives in a house made of sticks, called a lodge.

Did you know?
All the bees in a hive are related. A single queen bee is the mother of them all.

Who takes care of baby fish?

Most fish don't look after their eggs at all. The babies must find their own food as soon as they hatch. A few fish, however, do take care of their babies:

The **tilapia** holds her eggs in her mouth until they hatch. She can't eat anything for a week! After the eggs hatch, the mother lets the tiny fish swim back into her mouth when danger is near.

A **catfish** mother and father
guard their eggs together.
After the eggs hatch,
the parents take turns
feeding and caring
for the baby fish.

Why does a bird sit on its eggs?

To keep them warm so they will hatch. Before you were born, you stayed warm inside your mother's body. But bird eggs are laid outside, where it is cold. That's why a grown-up bird must keep its eggs snug and warm beneath its body.

Did you know?
An emperor penguin father warms his eggs by holding them on the tops of his feet, under a soft flap of skin.

Why do opossums carry their babies in pouches?

Because the babies are so small when they're born, their mother has to keep them warm. She also has to keep them safe from other animals. A pouch is a perfect place for the babies to hide and ride until they get bigger.

Did you know?

Kangaroos and koalas have pouches, too.
The babies drink milk from their mothers
while they are in the pouch. The milk
helps them grow.

Do all twins look alike?

Twins are two people who were born at the same time. If they look alike, they are called identical twins. But not all twins look like each other. Fraternal twins may look completely different. Sometimes fraternal twins are both boys, sometimes they are both girls, and sometimes they are one girl and one boy.

Was Daddy ever a baby?

Every person you know—your father, your mother, even your grandparents—was once a little baby. All animals were babies, too. Dogs were puppies, cats were kittens, cows were calves. Do you know what a baby kangaroo is called? A joey!

Try it!

What do you think your parents looked like when they were little? Ask your mother or father to show you pictures of themselves at your age.

41

How long does it take to grow up?

It doesn't take long for animals to grow up, but people take about 20 years or so. Children start out as babies. Then they grow bigger, and later on they are old enough to go to school. When children become teenagers, they are almost as big as grownups, but they still live at home. When they can take care of themselves without any help, they are all grown up.

What is a wedding?

A wedding is a celebration that takes place when a man and a woman get married. The man is called the groom, and the woman is called the bride. At the wedding, they promise to love each other and live together. It's a happy day for all their family and friends.

Did you know?
At some weddings, the groom stomps on a glass wrapped in cloth—that's for good luck. The guests may throw rice or birdseed at the bride and groom.

Will Mommy and Daddy still be my parents when I grow up?

Your mother and father will always be your parents. They will love you even when you get to be as big as they are. Even when you have your own children, your mother and father will still be your parents. Your brothers and sisters will always be your brothers and sisters, too. You'll have your family forever.

TIME-LIFE for CHILDREN®

MANAGING EDITOR: Patricia Daniels
EDITORIAL DIRECTORS: Jean Burke Crawford, Allan Fallow,
  Karin Kinney, Sara Mark, Elizabeth Ward
EDITORIAL COORDINATOR: Marike van der Veen
EDITORIAL ASSISTANT: Mary Saxton
SENIOR COPYEDITOR: Colette Stockum
SUPERVISOR OF QUALITY CONTROL: James King
LIBRARY: Louise D. Forstall
SPECIAL CONTRIBUTOR: Barbara Klein
WRITER: Jacqueline A. Ball

DESIGNED BY: David Bennett Books
SERIES DESIGN: David Bennett
BOOK DESIGN: David Bennett
ART DIRECTION: David Bennett & Andrew Crowson
ILLUSTRATED BY: Stuart Trotter
ADDITIONAL COVER ILLUSTRATIONS BY: Nick Baxter

Second printing. Printed in U.S.A.

TIME-LIFE is a trademark of Time Warner Inc. and affiliated companies.

School and library distribution by Time-Life Education, P.O. Box 85026,
Richmond, Virginia 23285-5026.

Library of Congress Cataloging-in-Publication Data
Do mommies have mommies? : first questions and answers about families.
  p. cm.—(Time-Life library of first questions and answers)

ISBN 0-7835-0877-8
1. Family—Miscellanea—Juvenile literature. [1. Family—Miscellanea.
 2. Questions and answers.]   I. Time-Life for Children (Firm) II. Series:
Library of first questions and answers.
HQ744.D64   1994
306.85—dc20   94-1946
                                                                  CIP
                                                                   AC

CONSULTANTS

Dr. Lewis P. Lipsitt, an internationally recognized specialist on childhood development, was the 1990 recipient of the Nicholas Hobbs Award for science in the service of children. He has served as the science director for the American Psychological Association and is a professor of psychology and medical science at Brown University, where he is director of the Child Study Center.

Thomas D. Mullin directs the Beaver Brook Association in Hollis, New Hampshire, where he coordinates workshops and seminars designed to promote appreciation for wildlife and the environment.

Dr. Judith A. Schickedanz, an authority on the education of preschool children, is an associate professor of early childhood education at the Boston University School of Education, where she also directs the Early Childhood Learning Laboratory. Her published work includes *More Than the ABC's: Early Stages of Reading and Writing Development* as well as several textbooks and many scholarly papers.